Affirmations for Black Boys
Daily Affirmations for Black Boys
to Build Confidence, Inspire and Increase Motivation
by Reprogramming Your Mind with Positive Affirmations.

D1518459

SIMPLE CODE
PUBLISHING

Affirmations for Black Boys

By Nathen Hughes

United States
2022

CONTENTS

INTRODUCTION: THE POTENTIAL OF BLACK BOYS?

As a former teacher, I know how much a kind word can brighten a child's day. I've also seen kids talk badly to themselves, which is very sad to see. Affirmations that are positive for black boys can really change how they feel about themselves. I can think of one student in particular. Brandon was having trouble in all of his classes in the third grade. He was cool to the other little boys. So, when he kept calling himself stupid and stopped doing his work, what do you think happened? Yes, it wasn't long before other little boys started calling themselves "idiot" and "stupid," too. One day, I got down on my knees next to his desk and told him, "Brandon, you can do it. You don't learn to read and write as quickly as some kids, but you have a great voice. I know you'll have a masterpiece if you write down the songs you've been practicing in the hallways. "He started to write down that song. He didn't think it was a masterpiece, but that was enough to keep him writing. It gave him the confidence he needed to keep writing songs. By the end of the year, he was at least willing to TRY working on the real daily assignment, which was never a song. I don't know what went through Abel's mind after that. Maybe he got through class every morning by telling himself nice things about his singing. So, let me start with my first point.

I'm not a therapist or psychologist, but there's a lot of evidence that positive affirmations for black boys do help the average person. Your brain sometimes gets confused about what's real and what's made up, which can be surprisingly helpful. The idea is that if you can just imagine being great, you can start to act on that idea and move toward being great. Take action. Obviously, just because you say something over and over, it doesn't mean it's true. But it CAN give you the way of thinking you need to reach your goal. Let's go back to Brandon, the student I talked about. Nothing would have happened if Abel had just kept repeating my compliment that he was a great singer. Still, he had to pull out that pencil and start writing. If an affirmation can change the way you think about something, that's a pretty good starting point. Positive affirmations can only go so far. If your child or student is having trouble with anxiety or depression, I think you will need to do more. To see big changes, these students need real medical help or therapy.

AFFIRMATIONS

1. I am worthy.
2. I am loved.
3. I am my only limit.
4. I am as good as anyone else.
5. My brown skin is beautiful, and it even absorbs sunlight!
6. I come from a long, rich Black heritage.
7. I only answer to what I want to be called.
8. I can try out every answer choice before circling one.
9. It's going to feel so good to try my best.
10. I will take my time.
11. If I get confused, I'll read it again.
12. I can try new things with a smile on my face.
13. I can be brave, even when I'm scared.
14. My mistakes help me learn and grow.
15. If at first, I don't succeed, I can try again.
16. I'm tough and I can get through anything.
17. When I step outside my comfort zone, I get braver each time!
18. My body is strong.
19. My body is growing all the time.
20. I can take care of my body and learn what it needs.
21. This is the body God gave me, and God doesn't make mistakes.
22. I can do the right thing, no matter what everyone else is doing.
23. My ideas are important.
24. I can change the world.
25. I can stand up for my beliefs.
26. I can help other people and make a difference.
27. I see the good in other people.
28. I can choose to forgive other people.
29. I can name my emotions and be okay with what I'm feeling.

30. I can be calm.

31. I can enjoy nature and be quiet.

32. I can choose peace and ignore chaos.

33. I am becoming more like Jesus every day.

34. God loves me just the way I am.

35. I can develop wisdom.

36. I can pray to God whenever and however I want.

37. God listens to me.

38. God wants what's best for me.

39. I can trust in God's plan for my life, even when I'm scared.

40. I can be anything I want to be.

41. I am strong and can do anything I set my mind to.

42. I am tough.

43. I can change if I want to.

44. The person I will be tomorrow is not the kid I used to be.

45. I have enough to be happy.

46. I'm grateful for what I have been given.

47. I have everything I need.

48. I can share what I have with other kids.

49. I have people who love me very much.

50. It's okay to feel what I'm feeling.

51. Having a good cry is a healthy thing.

52. I can yell into a pillow when I'm mad.

53. God can handle my anger if I'm mad at him.

54. It's normal to be afraid or worried sometimes.

55. I can say how I'm feeling out loud.

56. My feelings are not bigger than I am.

57. I can take care of my friends.

58. I can tell the truth with kindness.

59. I am an encourager.

60. I can surround myself with positive people.

61. I will help my friends make good choices.

62. I can be a great friend.

63. I can be happy when other kids have success.

64. I am a caring person.

65. I am a great listener.

66. I can solve problems respectfully.

67. I can keep a secret.

68. I am proud to be Black.

69. I make a difference

70. My hair is the perfect halo for my head

71. I'm allowed to take up space

72. I deserve love

73. I deserve respect

74. I embrace the greatness within me

75. My mental health matters

76. I am capable

77. My mind is full of brilliant ideas

78. My hair is the perfect crown

79. I inhale confidence and exhale doubt

80. I am so proud of who I am

81. I believe in me

82. I am powerful

83. I light the world with my smile

84. My confidence is beautiful

85. I am loved

86. I am a leader

87. I am dedicated to achieving my goals

88. I am beautiful

89. I am magical

90. I trust my inner guide

91. I am creatively inspired by the world around me

92. I accept myself

93. I am caring to others

94. I will speak kindly to myself

95. I am funny

96. I am Handsome

97. I am a magnet for blessings

98. My body is celestial

99. I am confident

100. I am brave

101. I am helpful

102. I will step out of my comfort zone and try something new today

103. I will allow peace to fill my soul

104. I am imperfect and perfectly me

105. I am smart

106. I release myself from my anger

107. The world has a need for me

108. I choose to be proud of myself

109. I choose my attitude

110. I am becoming healthier each and every day

111. I believe in myself

112. I am confident that I am able to conquer the world

113. I make good choices

114. I trust myself

115. I am brilliant

116. I deserve good things

117. I am a good friend

118. I will recognize my good qualities

119. I own my magic

120. I am kind

121. I am thankful for life

122. I am thoughtful

123. I love myself!

124. I will love myself unconditionally

125. Today is a new day; I will see what adventure it holds

126. It's okay to rest

127. I am revolutionary

128. I will do my best with whatever comes my way

129. I'm in charge of my future

130. My future is my own

131. Today is a new day!

132. I am thankful for today

133. I can make this a great day

134. I am courageous

135. I am unstoppable

136. My hard work is already paying off

137. I am so special

138. I release all fear from my mind

139. I learn from my mistakes

140. Nothing can steal my joy

141. I am evolving

142. I am filled with joy, happiness, and love

143. I know it can get tough out there, but I know I am designed for greatness – Danai Gurira

144. I can accomplish anything I set my mind to

145. I have the power to create change

146. I am better than I was yesterday

147. I love me for simply being

148. I will learn from yesterday and live for today

149. I am helpful

150. My brown skin is beautiful

151. I am important to my community

152. I am wise

153. I am understanding

154. I am loved

155. I make a difference in the world by simply existing in it

156. I am grateful to have people in my life who [fill in the blank]

157. I am becoming closer to my true self every day

For mothers & fathers to black son's

158. I am happy you are here

159. You add to this space

160. I love when you are happy!

161. Your hair is perfect however way you wear it

162. You are more than enough

163. I am so proud of who you are

164. You always have a choice

165. You are thoughtful

166. You are beautiful inside and out

167. Your ancestors are always with you

168. You are loved

169. I appreciate the energy you bring to this group

170. You are thoughtful

171. I believe in you

172. You are a problem solver

173. You are capable

174. I trust you will make the right decision, and if you don't- that's okay too. I will help you try again.

175. You make such great decisions.

176. I love the energy you bring to this space.

177. I'm so happy to see you!

178. Thanks for being here.

179. Thank you for sharing.

180. I love the way your mind works or I love the way you think.

181. You should be so proud of yourself.

182. You are brilliant.

183. Is it okay if I join you?

184. Thank you for sharing your space with me.

185. Thank you for allowing me to teach you.

186. Your opinion/feelings/beliefs matter to me.

187. I hear you.

188. I'm sorry. It will not happen again. (Do not by any means break this trust).

189. I don't know the answer to that. Can we figure it out together?

190. We can find a solution.

191. How can I support you?

192. I'm here to support you.

193. What do you need?

194. What do you think?

195. I'm here if you want to talk <u>and/or</u> I'm here if you'd like me to sit with you.

196. Do you need space?

197. Would you like a break?

198. It's okay to be angry.

199. I love being your teacher/nanny/mom/etc.,

200. What do you want to learn about?

201. I love your ideas/you have great ideas.

202. How you feel is important to me.

203. Trust yourself.

204. I see/appreciate the effort you put into this.

205. Thank you for participating.

206. It is okay to rest.

207. I appreciate you.

208. I'd really value your opinion/thoughts/feelings on this.

209. I'm so proud of who you are!

210. I am a leader
211.   I am creative
212.   I am valuable
213.   Everyday I get better
214.   I am full wealth
215.   My attitude is full of gratitude
216.   I am very helpful
217.   Happiness flows within me
218.   I am destined for greatness
219.   My voice is POWERFUL
220.   I believe in myself
221.   My mind is full of knowledge
222.   I am kind
223.   I love my mother
224.   I love my father
225.   I have great ideas
226.   I am capable
227.   Everyday I get better
228.   I am beautiful
229.   I believe in myself
230.   I'm allowed to take up space
231.   My confidence is inspiring
232.   I am in charge of my own destiny
233.   I am filled with joy
234.   I can accomplish my goals
235.   I make good choices
236.   I am incredibly special
237.   I am perfect just the way I am
238.   I am worthy
239.   I am magical
240.   I am thankful for today
241.   I am smart
242.   My future is bright
243.   I am unstoppable
244.   I learn from my mistakes

245.   I am creative
246.   I invite peace into my life
247.   I am my only limit
248.   I am proud to be Black
249.   My hair is the halo of my head
250.   I am kind
251.   My hair is the perfect crown
252.   I can do anything I put my mind to
253.   Happiness flows within me
254.   I deserve respect
255.   I trust myself
256.   I am unique
257.   I am wonderfully made
258.   I am valuable
259.   I can do hard things
260.   I have an attitude of gratitude
261.   I am a leader
262.   I am destined for greatness
263.   I make a difference
264.   I speak kindly to myself
265.   I deserve love
266.   I have the power to create change
267.   My mind is filled with knowledge
268.   My mental health matters
269.   I am so proud of who I am
270.   My brown skin is beautiful
271.   I am thoughtful
272.   I am brave
273.   I deserve good things
274.   I come from a long, rich Black heritage
275.   I am very helpful
276.   I am not afraid to stand out
277.   I light the world with my smile
278.   Today is a new day
279.   I'm a great friend
280.   The world has a need for me

281.   I have a POWERFUL voice
282.   It is important that I exist.
283.   To me, my beliefs are critical.
284.   My opinion counts.
285.   The decisions I make have far-reaching consequences, but I'm confident I'm making the best ones.
286.   Only by altering my own perspective can I bring about a revolution in society.
287.   I won't put up with being pushed around.
288.   As I progress in my career, I hope to improve my current performance.
289.   When I talk about my ideas with other people, we can make a difference.
290.   When I use my special skills to help others, the world will be a better place.
291.   Because I am deserving of joy, I am surrounded by joy, laughter, peace, and abundance.
292.   I do not just exist without purpose in this world. The world is a better place because of me, and I know that.
293.   In today's world, I will not be a failure.
294.   The keys to my success, or failure, lie in my own hands.
295.   I have the fortitude and skill to overcome any obstacle I face.
296.   Insofar as I take care of myself and listen to my inner voice, I won't need any other guidance.
297.   I am confident in my abilities and derive pleasure from surprising people.
298.   I can teach myself anything if I put in the effort.
299.   Having confidence in myself does not rely solely on the opinions of others.
300.   I can overcome any obstacle.

301.   The things I'm afraid of are nothing I can't handle. I used to do that.

302. So long as I do what I need to, I'll be in a good place to flourish.

303. For the most part, I have been successful.

304. Having said that, I am confident.

305. When I speak, people listen.

306. I am mighty.

307. It seems like every day I make some sort of improvement.

308. The resources I require are already within me.

309. When I first open my eyes in the morning, I feel inspired.

310. To put it simply, I am a tornado that can't be stopped.

311. My very existence serves as a demonstration of the power of inspiration.

312. This is a time of great prosperity for me.

313. The people I interact with are being uplifted and encouraged by me.

314. Through my work, I am able to encourage others.

315. I am not going to give in to the negative emotions or thoughts that have been trying to control my mind.

316. What a fantastic day it is today.

317. At the same time that I am turning up the positive in my life, I am turning down the negative.

318. My mind is laser-focused.

319. My problems don't drive me; my aspirations do.

320. I appreciate everything that God has provided for me.

321. I'm able to take care of myself and don't need anyone else.

322. What I am depends entirely on my own desires.

323. What motivates me is not my past, but rather my potential in the future.

324. The challenges I face push me to improve and broaden my horizons.

325. A lot of work will get done today.

326.   Intelligent and determined best describe me.

327.   Every day, my sense of gratitude grows.

328.   The passing days have allowed me to gradually recover my health.

329.   I am getting closer and closer to my objectives with each passing day.

330.   Weird things are happening to me and around me right now, and it's all because of the power of my thoughts and words.

331.   I am continually developing into a more admirable person.

332.   I'm releasing all of the negative self-doubt and fear that's been holding me back.

333.   By embracing my uniqueness, I am able to cultivate inner calm, strength, and self-assurance.

334.   To set myself free, I must first forgive myself. In return for your forgiveness, please forgive me.

335.   Day by day, I feel better and stronger.

336.   Not a single day of my life goes to waste. I make the most of every moment of today, tomorrow, and every day of my life.

337.   Keep in mind the tremendous strength I have within me to accomplish anything.

338.   I have a place here, and I am valued by those who know me.

339.   Even though I have a dreadful history, I am a stunning woman now.

340.   Mistakes I've made are not who I am.

341.   My inner glow warms the hearts of those around me.

342.   I'm allowed to feel human, and crying is one of those things.

343.   and to grieve, to feel disappointment, to feel shame, to make mistakes, to fail, to laugh, and to cry.

344.   sing my praises, and I'll finally be able to fully embrace my humanity and bask in all its splendor.

345. As a dwelling place for God, my physical form is nothing short of a work of art.
346. I am a product of the skill of his hands.
347. The sun's rays have touched my skin, and I feel slightly warmer as a result.
348. In a sky full of stars, I stand out as Polaris; my presence will be honored; I am revered.
349. Rather than being another discarded black body, you should refuse to be one.
350. I will give myself permission to change and grow;
351. I will have faith in my method and give myself credit for my achievements.
352. I am trying, and I will accept that as sufficient.
353. Even though I am not perfect, I am aware of my many redeeming features.
354. I'm going to make it anyway.
355. I will not give in to my foes;
356. This self-love I cultivate will be the source of peace in my life.
357. No matter what comes my way, I will not be uprooted from the solid foundation of selfless love.
358. I will never doubt my abilities or diminish my expectations of myself.
359.
360. I accept and appreciate myself just the way I am.
361.
362. When it comes to my own judgment, I have complete faith in myself.
363. With each stride I take, I become more powerful.
364. Whatever I put my mind to, I will accomplish.
365. That I am powerful and capable.
366. No challenge is too great for me to overcome.
367. I take deep breaths of assurance and release my worries.
368. The emotion of fear is fleeting. I am able to take action despite anxiety.

369.   By letting go of my doubt, I make way for success.
370.   I'm not shy about talking to new people; in fact, I thrive on it.
371.   When it comes to my own worth and beauty, I am completely satisfied.
372.   It's important to me to focus on the here and now, but I also have faith in the future.
373.   An air of self-assurance permeates everything I do.
374.   I like to think of myself as an outgoing and confident person.
375.   My independence, originality, and tenacity serve me well in any endeavor.
376.   I have a lot of vitality and excitement. I've always been a confident person.
377.   Everything that happens to me is for the best, and I only attract positive and happy experiences.
378.   I enjoy figuring out complicated issues and helping others do the same.
379.   By putting my mind to it, I always come up with the best solution.
380.   I am very adaptable, and I enjoy being thrust into unfamiliar situations.
381.   I thrive when tested. Because of them, I am able to shine brighter than I ever have before.
382.   Everything is within my reach.
383.   In order to succeed today, I am prepared to fail.
384.   I'm very pleased with my effort to even try this.
385.   I have taken good care of myself and can confidently say that I am healthy and well-groomed.
386.   My health on the outside is paralleled by my internal peace.
387.   I function best when I am assured of my own abilities.
388.   There is no such thing as an impossible task.
389.   There is no bad in anyone else's eyes in mine.
390.   Positive people are drawn to me.

391.   I am confident and brave in the face of adversity.

392.   There are no conditions attached to my self-love and acceptance.

393.   The world owes me a favor because I am a worthy human being.

394.   In general, I like and approve of myself very highly.

395.   Respect and adoration are returned to me in equal measure.

396.   People really care about me and respect me.

397.   Thanks to my lofty sense of self-worth, I am able to respect others and to be respected in return.

398.   My goals are achievable because I am strong enough to achieve them.

399.   It's up to me to decide what to do.

400.   You should hold me in high regard because I am a one-of-a-kind, very special human being.

401.   Everyday, I grow more and more fond of who I am as a person.

402.   As a result of my healthy sense of self-worth, I am able to take compliments in stride.

403.   When I accept people for who they are, they do the same for me.

404.   What other people think is irrelevant. The only thing that matters is my response and my opinion.

405.   When I give and receive love and acceptance, the world rewards me.

406.   I value myself highly, so I feel good about myself.

407.   That's right, I came out on top.

408.   That which is good in the world is mine due.

409.   There is no longer any requirement for your pain and anguish.

410.   I let go of the need to prove myself to anyone because I am already complete and that's perfect for me!

411.   I always try to find a workable answer.

412.   There is always a way to deal with whatever issue arises.

413.	I am never completely alone. Everything in the cosmos is on my side and rooting for me.
414.	Thoughts of love, health, positivity, and success fill my head with ideas, which I then translate into actual events.
415.	I am Incredibly blessed, my thoughts are filled with thanksgiving.
416.	The choice to be self-assured is mine today and every day.
417.	I radiate confidence, certainty and optimism
418.	When presented with a chance, I don't hesitate to boldly push it open and take advantage of it.
419.	Every aspect of my life is planned out by me.
420.	I can make my dreams a reality.
421.	Imagination is all I need to achieve anything.
422.	I speak up for my convictions.
423.	I take bold, sure steps.
424.	I have faith in myself.
425.	I like to think outside the norm and have an imaginative mind.
426.	My thoughts and plans always end up well for me.
427.	In the morning, I get up and do something that matters.
428.	Every day, my company expands.
429.	This thing I'm making is bigger than me.
430.	Currently, I am living out my life's mission.
431.	Forgive me, I utterly fail
432.	No longer do I have to let my past define me;
433.	I get to make my own future from here on out.
434.	I release my anger and hatred toward those who have wronged me.
435.	Those who have wronged me in the past are forgiven, and I am at peace with myself again.
436.	With all three, my life is abundant.
437.	Each new door I walk through is replete with possibilities and benefits.

438. It seems that the more I give to others, the more they give back to me.
439. Current activities help me achieve my ultimate goals.
440. Anytime I want, I can instantly alter the way I'm thinking.
441. What I do with my life is entirely up to me.
442. It is within my control to make positive changes.
443. Having fun and enjoying life is something I allow myself to do.
444. Because of me, the world is better.
445. There is nothing that has happened or will happen that has upset me.
446. This is only the start of my life.
447. I'm making a conscious decision today to replace my negative routines with more constructive ones.
448. I'm so thankful that I was able to kick my vices.
449. I have finally broken my addictions.
450. I only engage in good routines.
451. I am grateful for the opportunity to see another day.
452. I have a colorful and lovely view of the world.
453. Whatever good happens to me today is entirely deserved.
454. There are many doors of possibility opening for me today, and I am ready to welcome them in.
455. I make an effort to show my close friends how much they mean to me.
456. The good things that happen to me are a direct result of the good vibes I put out into the world.
457. I'm just chilling out and seeing where life takes me.
458. Yes, I will choose joy today and every day.
459. People enjoy being around me because I am lively and upbeat.
460. The joy and love in my life are endless.
461. Nothing ever stands in the way of my joy.

462.   Sustaining my mind with positive ideas is how I keep it going.
463.   Good nutrition is how I keep myself going.
464.   I fuel myself with nutritious foods.
465.   Exercising keeps my head and body fueled.
466.   In every way, my body is getting healthier by the day.
467.   I feel healthier and more energized by the day.
468.   I am a leader in every sense of the word.
469.   An Inspiring Leader Is Me
470.   Other people look up to me as a model
471.   I motivate people to become their best selves.
472.   As a leader, I always try to set a good example.
473.   I have the ability to convey my ideas clearly and concisely.
474.   For as much as I love the world, it loves me right back.
475.   I make the decision to share with others today and every day.
476.   I make the decision to improve the world today, and every day.
477.   I see love everywhere I turn.
478.   As a result, my immediate circle is always full of cheery, supportive souls.
479.   This is the day I might finally meet the one.
480.   Ready for love: I am
481.   Over time, my feelings for myself have only grown.
482.   Both my family and my friends are incredible blessings in my life.
483.   It never seems to be a problem for me to find adequate funds.
484.   Money comes to me like a glistening river of gold.
485.   Seeing my savings expand is a joy.
486.   Many of my thoughts revolve around how to make a profit.
487.   My salary keeps going up and up.

488.   The amount of money I give away is always multiplied back to me.
489.   Currently, I am laying claim to my portion.
490.   I am blessed with a steady stream of income.
491.   I have earned a comfortable lifestyle
492.   I thrive on being pushed to my limits because it forces me to develop.
493.   Every event in my life has taught me something and provided me with a chance to grow.
494.   Each day, my outlook becomes more positive and healthier.
495.   My timing is impeccable, and I never miss a crucial opportunity.
496.   I am equipped to handle this difficulty.
497.   As a result of overcoming obstacles, I have grown as a person.
498.   Every experience has helped me develop and expand.
499.   The current events are working out for my highest good.
500.   I've made a conscious effort to replace my bad routines with more productive ones.
501.   Every day, I am able to accomplish more.
502.   I am extremely self-disciplined, and that is why I will ultimately be successful.
503.   Because I am willing to put in more effort than anyone else, I always come out on top.
504.   I refuse to give up until it's my last breath.
505.   I make efficient use of my time because I know how precious it is.
506.   The work that I do is always disciplined and fruitful on my part.
507.   I consider myself to be the most attractive person in my social circle.
508.   In short, I'm a good person who wants to show the world how good my heart is.

509. I am currently in a position of complete autonomy in which to make a choice about my next course of action.

510. I was sent here as a present to the world.

511. I am special and have a lot to give to the world.

512. I am the epitome of sexiness.

513. I can decide whether to accept or reject an offer.

514. Daily, I make a conscious decision to focus on what really matters to me.

515. My decision to succeed today, and every day, is a conscious one.

516. I am not driven by desperation, but rather by inspiration when making decisions.

517. Good fortune and achievement seem to be drawn to me.

518. I've grown both physically and mentally since yesterday.

519. That's right, I'm a genius and I use my knowledge in my daily life.

520. Success-minded, like-minded people are drawn to me like a magnet.

521. I'm increasing in success every day, in every way.

522. Because of how I was raised, I always expect to be happy and successful.

523. In every endeavor, I give my all and achieve the highest standards.

524. Possibilities and rewards abound in my exciting and thrilling life.

525. I will not stray from my path

526. Issues? I've got answers.

527. I am getting closer to my objectives every day, and especially today.

528. I have identified my higher purpose and am working toward it.

529. I have a job that matters and makes a difference in the world.

530. I'm willing to try new things.

531. I am the definition of success
532. I have earned my success.
533. Just being myself is the best option available.
534. That suffices for me.
535. Daily, I make more progress toward my goal.
536. My character is unparalleled.
537. Each of my issues can be fixed.
538. I am a leader now.
539. For my part, I've accepted responsibility for my shortcomings and apologize to myself.
540. The difficulties I face force me to develop as a person.
541. No changes need to be made to me because I am perfect as I am.
542. Learning from my errors aids my development.
543. Things are looking up for today.
544. The confidence and bravery I possess is unwavering.
545. The level of joy I experience is entirely under my control.
546. I am surrounded by people who adore and value me.
547. I'm not afraid to fight for my convictions.
548. The things I hope to accomplish inspire me.
549. It's fine to admit ignorance sometimes.
550. I'm going to try to have a good attitude today.
551. Everything will not break me.
552. If I set my mind to it, I can accomplish any goal.
553. To exercise personal agency, I now grant myself permission.
554. Next time, I'll be more prepared.
555. Right now, I don't need anything else.
556. I can accomplish a lot.
557. There is no need to worry; everything will be fine.
558. When I say something, I mean it.

559. To put it simply, I am pleased with my own accomplishments.
560. I have earned the right to joy.
561. Yes, I can choose whatever I want to do.
562. I am deserving of love.
563. Yes, I can affect change.
564. To put it simply, I am going to be confident today.
565. For the first time in my life, I feel in control.
566. To make my goals a reality is within my control.
567. To put it simply, I have faith in my own skills and abilities.
568. I believe only good things are in store for me.
569. It is important that I exist.
570. As soon as I leave the house, I feel a surge of self-assurance.
571. I'm going to face my fears head-on today.
572. I'm eager to take in new information.
573. Each day is a new beginning.
574. Even if I do fail, I know I can always try again.
575. All of the pieces of me fit together perfectly.
576. The only person I can honestly judge my progress against is myself.
577. I'm capable of anything.

Final Thoughts

This was Affirmations for black boys.
These affirmations not only help us overcome negative thinking and delay tactics, but they also inspire us to perform at our highest potential, hone our skills, and realize our ambitions.

Trust me when I say, my prince, this collection of the best affirmations is your secret weapon for a stellar start to the day.

Let's make a conscious effort to repeat these affirmations in order to enhance our confidence and love our flaws.

Don't forget to leave a comment in the review box with your favorite powerful quote.

THE END

Made in the USA
Monee, IL
29 May 2023

34892666R00020